The
Miracle

Scan the QR code to see the music video of
"The Miracle" by Shawna Belt Edwards.

All art by Sandra Rast and Julie Rogers. For print information on Sandra's art, please go to sandrarast.com. For print information on Julie's art, please go to julierogersart.com.

Cover image: *King of Love, My Shepherd* © Julie Rogers

Image right: *Presidence of Faith* © Sandra Rast

Music and Words by Shawna Belt Edwards. For more information on Shawna's music, go to shawnaedwardsmusic.com.

Cover and interior designed by Christina Marcano

Cover design copyright © 2021 Covenant Communications, Inc.

Published by Covenant Communications, Inc.

American Fork, Utah

Printed in the United States of America

First Printing: March 2021

27 26 25 24 23 22 21   10 9 8 7 6 5 4 3 2 1

ISBN: 978-1-52440-977-7

The Miracle

Written by Shawna Belt Edwards ∾ Art by Julie Rogers and Sandra Rast

Jesus walked
upon the water;

He stilled the storm
and calmed the angry sea.

With *His* hands,

He healed the leper;

He made the lame to walk,

the blind to see.

$\mathcal{H}e$ fed a thousand people
with a loaf or two of bread,

and when the ruler's daughter died,
He **raised** her from the dead.

Jesus bled and

died to *save me* -

A price that

I could never pay alone.

When He rose again,

He gave me

the ***greatest*** gift

the world has ever known.

Yes, I can
be *forgiven*
every time
that I repent,

And someday

He will lift me up

to *live* with

Him again.

I *know* He will walk

beside me

and heal my wounds
and calm my troubled heart.

Every day, He'll bless and guide me

and make me clean if I will do my part.

His love and mercy never end;

each morning, they are new.

My name is graven on His *hands*,

and yours is too.

Jesus is a God of
miracles.

Nothing is at all

impossible to Him.

But I know this:
Of all *His* miracles,

The most
incredible

must be

the miracle

that rescues me.

The Miracle

SHAWNA BELT EDWARDS

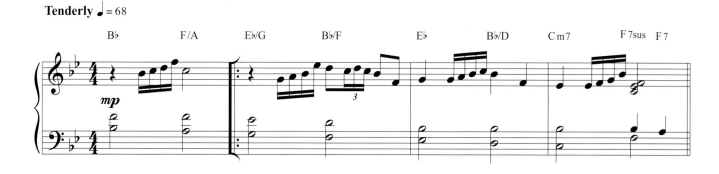

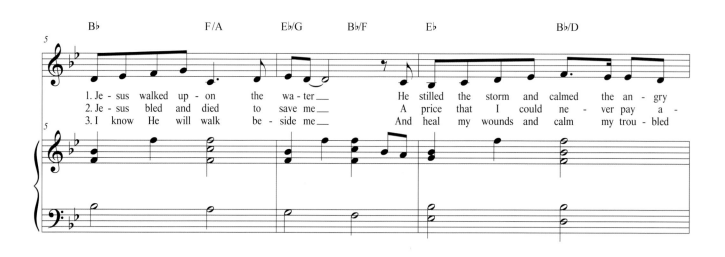

1. Je - sus walked up - on the wa - ter___ He stilled the storm and calmed the an - gry
2. Je - sus bled and died to save me___ A price that I could ne - ver pay a -
3. I know He will walk be - side me___ And heal my wounds and calm my trou - bled

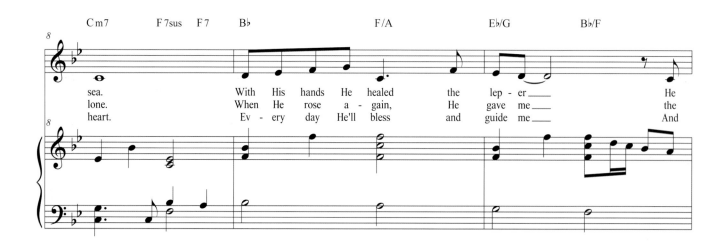

sea. With His hands He healed the lep - er___ He
lone. When He rose a - gain, He gave me___ the
heart. Ev - ery day He'll bless and guide me___ And

made the lame to walk, the blind to see.
He fed a thou-sand peo-ple with a
great-est gift the world has e-ver known.
Yes, I can be for-giv-en ev-ery
make me clean if I will do my part.
His love and grace will ne-ver end; Each

loaf or two of bread, and when the rul-er's daugh-ter died, __ He raised her from the dead. _____
time that I re-pent, and some day He will lift me up __ to live with Him a-gain. _____
mor-ning they are new. My name is grav-en on His hands, And yours is too. _____

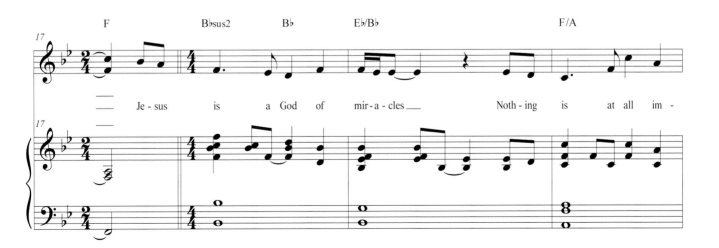

__ Je-sus is a God of mir-a-cles __ Noth-ing is at all im-

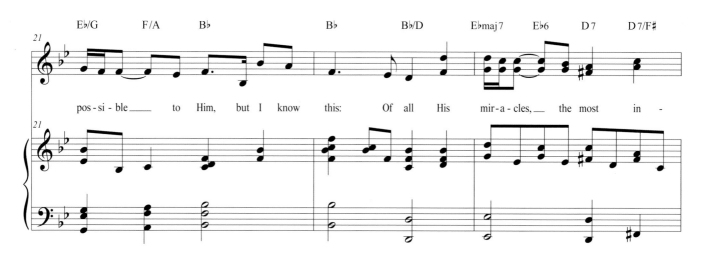

pos-si-ble_____ to Him, but I know this: Of all His mir-a-cles,_____ the most in-

cred-i-ble_____ must be the mir-a-cle_____ that res-cues me.

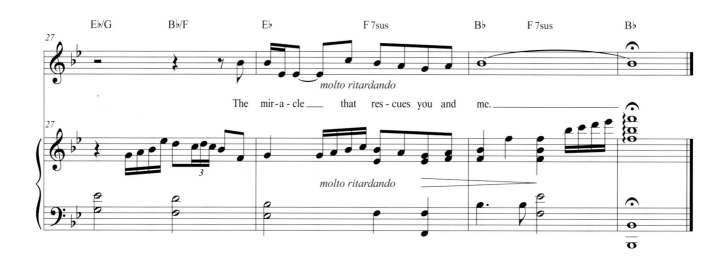

molto ritardando

The mir-a-cle_____ that res-cues you and me. _____

molto ritardando